MW01073932

CMMC SIMPLIFIED

The beginner's guide to understanding CMMC

Fernando Machado

Table of Contents

Table of Contents i

The CMMC Five Stages of Grief 1

Acronyms 3

Who 5

What: The CMMC Model 6

What: The CMMC Ecosystem 7

What: CUI 12

What: Tools 13

When 14

Where 15

Why 17

How 19

Summary 23

About the Author 24

The CMMC Five Stages of Grief

If you're reading this, it means you've heard about the Cybersecurity Maturity Model Certification (CMMC) but may not know much about it. I've decided to put together this easy-to-read guide on getting you caught up. Everything you need to know about the basics of the CMMC program in under 25 pages.

Before we begin, here are a few phrases I've heard throughout my CMMC consulting journey. I started categorizing them into the CMMC Five Stages of Grief.[1] If you're brave, take a shot of your favorite drink for each time you, or anyone you know, has said one of these phrases! 😁

Denial

- "We're a [SELECT ONE OR MORE: small; micro; mom & pop; disadvantaged; minority-owned; woman-owned; veteran-owned] business. It doesn't apply to us."

- "I'll just call my [SELECT ONE OR MORE: Congressman; Senator; Lobbyist] and makes this go away."

- "We're already [SELECT ONE OR MORE: AS9100; ISO 27001; SOC; PCI; HIPAA] certified/compliant."

- "I'll wait until it's in my contract."

- "CMMC is going away."

- "We're not in scope – it doesn't apply to us, just our client" (favorite line that comes from an MSP/MSSP with enterprise admin rights).

---

[1] Shoutout to Tom Cornelius at Compliance Forge™ for coming up with an early version of this list.

Anger

- "Why is the DoD doing this now?!"
- "I've been in business for [INSERT NUMBER] years!"
- "How long is this going to take?"
- "But it isn't in the contract!"

Bargaining

- "Our IT guys will take care of it."
- "We'll just put our data in the cloud."
- "Our managed service provider handles that/will handle that."
- "Can't we just accept the risk?"
- "I'm sure there will be waivers."

Depression

- "This is going to set us back."
- "Is DoD going to pay us to do this?"
- "I can't take this to my management?"

Acceptance

- "Let's schedule a time and discuss."
- "If this works, I can become a prime."
- "We will no longer do business with the DoD."

Since you're reading this book, you're probably in the '*Acceptance*' stage. Congratulations!

Acronyms

Now that we've got that out of the way, let's go over some common acronyms and their definitions you'll see throughout your CMMC journey:

- **CMMC – Cybersecurity Maturity Model Certification**

  o The Cybersecurity Maturity Model Certification (CMMC) program is aligned to DoD's information security for DIB partners. It is designed to enforce protection of sensitive unclassified information that is shared by the Department with its contractors and subcontractors. The program provides the Department increased assurance that contractors and subcontractors are meeting the cybersecurity requirements that apply to acquisition programs and systems that process controlled unclassified information.

- **CUI – Controlled Unclassified Information**

  o Controlled Unclassified Information (CUI) is information that requires safeguarding or dissemination controls pursuant to and consistent with applicable law, regulations, and government-wide policies but is not classified under Executive Order 13526 or the Atomic Energy Act, as amended.

- **DCMA DIBCAC – Defense Contract Management Agency Defense Industrial Base Cybersecurity Assessment Center**

  o Leads the DoD contractor cybersecurity risk mitigation efforts by assessing DoD contractors' compliance with the DFARS 252.204-7012, DFARS 252.204-7020, and NIST SP 800-171.

- **DFARS – Defense Federal Acquisition Regulation Supplement**

  o The Defense Federal Acquisition Regulation Supplement (DFARS) to the Federal Acquisition Regulation (FAR) is administered by the Department of Defense (DoD). The DFARS implements and supplements the FAR.

- **DoD – Department of Defense**
  - The Department of Defense provides the military forces needed to deter war, and to protect the security of the United States.

- **FAR – Federal Acquisition Regulation**
  - The Federal Acquisition Regulation (FAR) is the primary regulation for use by all executive agencies in their acquisition of supplies and services with appropriated funds.

- **FCI – Federal Contract Information**
  - Federal Contract Information means information, not intended for public release, that is provided by or generated for the Government under a contract to develop or delivery a product or service to the Government, but not including information provided by the Government to the public (such as on public websites) or simple transactional information, such as necessary to process payments.

- **NARA – National Archives and Records Administration**
  - The National Archives and Records Administration serves as the Executive Agent for the CUI Program.

- **POAM – Plan of Action and Milestones**
  - A document that identifies tasks that need to be accomplished. It details resources required to accomplish the elements of the plan, milestones for meeting the tasks, and the scheduled completion dates for the milestones.

- **SPRS – Supplier Performance Risk System**
  - Web enabled enterprise application that gathers, processes, and displays data about supplier performance.

Who

Question: Who is pushing CMMC?

Although CMMC is an effort led by the DoD, other agencies, organizations, and even other governments have begun adopting CMMC or "CMMC-type" language in their contractual agreements. For example:

- The Canadian government recently announced that they will be implementing something very similar to CMMC.

- The General Services Administration (GSA) included CMMC language in the 8(a) STARS III GWAC.

- United Launch Alliance (ULA) and other contractors are putting CMMC requirements in their contracts.

Question: Who will CMMC apply to?

Upon completion of rulemaking, CMMC will apply to contractors and subcontractors to the Department of Defense that process, store, and/or transmit Federal Contract Information (FCI) and/or Controlled Unclassified Information (CUI).

NIST SP 800-171 Paragraph 1.1: Purpose and Applicability states: "The requirements apply to components of nonfederal systems that process, store, or transmit CUI, or that provide security protection for such components." In other words, CMMC compliance *is likely* to involve managed service providers (MSP), managed security service providers (MSSP), cloud service providers (CSP), and more.

What: The CMMC Model

Question: What is CMMC?

Let's dive into the CMMC model. The CMMC model is *data centric*, meaning depending on the data that you're processing, storing, and/or transmitting, will determine which CMMC level you'll need to meet in the future. Contractors who fail to meet requirements will be unable to bid on contracts or maintain current contracts.

As of the writing of this publication, CMMC level 3 requirements are under development, and I did not include it to avoid confusion.

Data	CMMC Level	Number of Requirements	Security Requirements	Assessment Requirements
FCI	1	17	CMMC Level 1 Self-Assessment Guide	Self-assessment & annual affirmation
CUI	2	110	CMMC Level 2 Assessment Guide	3rd Party Assessments

Let's take the following example. Let's say you're a 3rd tiered subcontractor who has had the DFARS 252.204-7012 clause flowed down to you in a contractual agreement, and you're handling CUI. Per the chart above, you would need to meet the CMMC level 2 requirements.

What: The CMMC Ecosystem

The Cybersecurity Maturity Model Certification Accreditation Body (Cyber AB)[2] is the official accreditation body of the Cybersecurity Maturity Model Certification (CMMC) program. The Cyber AB was awarded a no-cost contract by the U.S. Department of Defense to implement and oversee the CMMC compliance ecosystem.

The CMMC ecosystem is divided into four primary roles:

- DIB Companies (OSCs)
- Consulting and Implementation
- Assessing and Certification; and
- Training and Instructors

---

[2] The Cyber AB name and Cyber AB logo are trademarks of the CMMC Accreditation Body.

- **DIB Companies**

Organization Seeking Certification (OSC) – The entity that is going through the CMMC assessment process to receive a level of certification for a given environment.

CMMC 3rd Party Assessment Organization (C3PAO)
Assessment Organization

Organization Seeking Certification (OSC)
Company

- **Consulting and Implementation**
  - *Registered Practitioner Organization (RPO)* – The Registered Practitioner Organization designation is designed for organizations that could provide services within the defense supply chain as an advisory firm or as an MSP (managed Service Provider). Think of them as the consulting firm.

  - *Registered Practitioner (RP)* – The Registered Practitioner program is training individuals on the following domains to assist OSC's in preparing for a CMMC assessment. Implementing the CMMC L1 framework. Think of them as the consultant working for the consulting firm.

  - *Registered Practitioner Advanced (RPA)* - The Registered Practitioner program is training individuals on the following domains to assist OSC's in preparing for a CMMC assessment. Implementing the CMMC L2 framework. Think of them as the consultant working for the consulting firm.

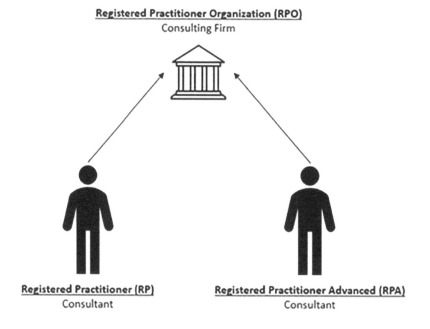

Registered Practitioner Organization (RPO)
Consulting Firm

Registered Practitioner (RP)
Consultant

Registered Practitioner Advanced (RPA)
Consultant

- **Assessing and Certification**
  - *CMMC 3rd Party Assessment Organization (C3PAO)* – An organization that has successfully passed a rigorous series of requirements to become acknowledged by the Cyber AB, on behalf of the DoD, as being objective and competent to perform assessments of OSC's.

  - *Certified CMMC Assessor (CCA)* – Preparing to become a CCA not only requires training and passing a high-stakes certification exam, but it also requires participation on three (3) level 2 assessments to gain the hands-on experience to become a Certified Level 2 assessor.

  - *Certified CMMC Professional (CCP)* – A person seeking to become responsible for the assessment, examination, verification, and review of an organization for compliance to a respective level of CMMC standards. A CCP is eligible to become a Certified CMMC Assessor, participates up to CMMC level 2 assessments, and holds a valuable credential reflecting the training to understand the CMMC requirements for a Defense supplier. Think of them as a junior assessor.

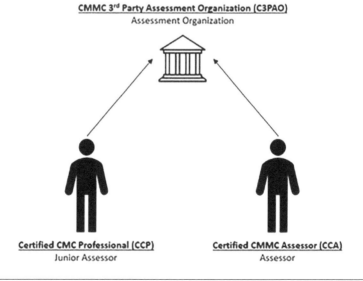

CMMC 3rd Party Assessment Organization (C3PAO)
Assessment Organization

Certified CMC Professional (CCP)
Junior Assessor

Certified CMMC Assessor (CCA)
Assessor

- **Training and Instructors**
  - *Licensed Training Provider (LTP)* – An established training organization that has been vetted by the Cybersecurity Assessor and Instruction Certification Organization (CAICO) to be approved as an LTP. Think of them as your training center.

  - *Licensed Publishing Partner (LPP)* – Responsible for creating quality CMMC training content that is utilized by the Licensed Training Providers (LTP's) to train individuals who are pursuing assessor or assessor instructor certifications.

  - *Provisional Instructor (PI)* – An individual responsible for teaching the CMMC framework to candidates seeking to be an assessor. This designation will be called Certified CMMC Instructor (CCI) in the future.

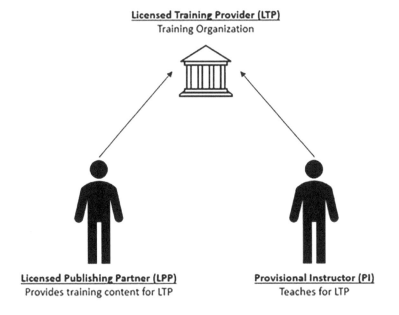

Licensed Training Provider (LTP)
Training Organization

Licensed Publishing Partner (LPP)
Provides training content for LTP

Provisional Instructor (PI)
Teaches for LTP

What: CUI

Have you ever asked yourself the aged-old question: what the f@*k is CUI? Although there are over 100 categories of CUI, most DoD contractors will only encounter two primary CUI types:

1. **Controlled Technical Information**
   a. Controlled Technical Information means technical information with military or space application that is subject to controls on the access, use, reproduction, modification, performance, display, release, disclosure, or dissemination. Controlled technical information is to be marked with one of the distribution statements B through F, in accordance with Department of Defense Instruction 5230.24, "Distribution Statements of Technical Documents." The term does not include information that is lawfully publicly available without restrictions. "Technical Information" means technical data or computer software, as those terms are defined in Defense Federal Acquisition Regulation Supplement clause 252.227-7013, "Rights in Technical Data - Noncommercial Items" (48 CFR 252.227-7013). Examples of technical information include research and engineering data, engineering drawings, and associated lists, specifications, standards, process sheets, manuals, technical reports, technical orders, catalog-item identifications, data sets, studies and analyses and related information, and computer software executable code and source code.

2. **Export Controlled**
   a. Unclassified information concerning certain items, commodities, technology, software, or other information whose export could reasonably be expected to adversely affect the United States national security and nonproliferation objectives. To include dual use items; items identified in export administration regulations, international traffic in arms regulations (ITAR) and the munitions list; license applications; and sensitive nuclear technology information.

What: Tools

Question: What free tools and resources can you use for your compliance journey?

The are several free government resources to help small businesses.

Here are a few tools to consider:

- **NSA Cybersecurity Collaboration Center** – The CCC works with industry, interagency, and international partners to harden the U.S. Defense Industrial Base, operationalize NSA's unique insights on nation-state cyber threats, jointly create mitigations guidance for emerging activity and chronic cybersecurity challenges, and secure emerging technologies. Here is their website: https://www.nsa.gov/About/Cybersecurity-Collaboration-Center/
- **NIST SP 800-171A** – The purpose of this publication is to provide procedures for assessing the CUI requirements in NIST SP 800-171. Here is their website: https://csrc.nist.gov/publications/detail/sp/800-171a/final
- **CMMC Level 2 Assessment Guide** – The CMMC Level 2 Assessment Guide provides assessment guidance for conducting CMMC assessments for Level 2. The CMMC Level 2 Assessment Guide combines the discussion paragraphs from NIST SP 800-171 and the assessment objectives from NIST SP 800-171A. Here is their website: https://dodcio.defense.gov/CMMC/
- **NIST SP 800-171 DoD Assessment Methodology, version 1.2.1** – Documents a standard methodology that enables a strategic assessment of a contractor's implementation of NIST SP 800-171, a requirement for compliance with DFARS clause 252.204-7012. Here is their website: https://www.acq.osd.mil/asda/dpc/cp/cyber/docs/safeguarding/NIST-SP-800-171-Assessment-Methodology-Version-1.2.1-6.24.2020.pdf

Question: When CMMC going to come live?

On May 16, 2023, DoD Chief Information Officer Honorable John Sherman stated, "We still don't have CMMC 2.0 out of the building yet because we're working to get it right. It's going to go to the Small Business Administration first and then into [the Office of Management and Budget] here in the hopefully very near future…rest assured we want to get this right."

Additionally, on May 18, 2023, DoD Deputy Chief Information Officer for Cybersecurity David McKeown stated the Pentagon is, "…really focused on DIB cybersecurity, and we continue to work on the [Cybersecurity Maturity Model Certification] (CMMC) rule. That's progressing pretty well inside the building. We're working through [Office of the General Counsel] (OGC) right now to get that out of the building, get it over to the Office of Small Business, and then follow up at [Office of Management and Budget] (OMB). We're targeting late fall of next year, so that can start to be put into contracts."

The Small Business Administration (SBA) has reviewed the CMMC rule and provided their comments due to its impact on small businesses.

On July 24, 2023, the CMMC rule has been sent to OMB for review. You can see the CMMC rule currently under review here: https://www.reginfo.gov/public/jsp/EO/eoDashboard.myjsp?agency_cd=0000&agency_nm=All&stage_cd=2&from_page=index.jsp&sub_index=0

Where

Question: Where does CMMC get its authority?

If you're processing, storing, and/or transmitting CUI, there are three clauses you need to be aware of:

1. **DFARS 252.204-7012 Safeguarding Covered Defense Information and Cyber Incident Reporting**
   a. DFARS 252.204-7012(b)(2)(i): "Except as provided in paragraph (b)(2)(ii) of this clause, the covered contractor information system shall be subject to the security requirements in National Institute of Standards and Technology (NIST) Special Publication (SP) 800-171, "Protecting Controlled Unclassified Information in Nonfederal Information Systems and Organizations" (available via the internet at http://dx.doi.org/10.6028/NIST.SP.800-171) in effect at the time the solicitation is issued or as authorized by the Contracting Officer."

   b. DFARS 252.204-7012(b)(2)(ii)(A): "*The Contractor shall implement NIST SP 800-171*, as soon as practical, but *not later than December 31, 2017*. For all contracts awarded prior to October 1, 2017, the Contractor shall notify the DoD Chief Information Officer (CIO), via email at osd.dibcsia@mail.mil, within 30 days of contract award, of any security requirements specified by NIST SP 800-171 not implemented at the time of contract award" (emphasis added)."

2. **DFARS 252.204-7019 Notice of NIST SP 800-171 DoD Assessment Requirements**
   a. DFARS 252.204-7019(b): "In order to be considered for award, if the Offeror is required to implement NIST SP 800-171, the Offeror shall have a current assessment (i.e., not more than 3 years old unless a lesser time is specified in the solicitation) (see 252.204-7020) for each covered contractor information system that is relevant to the offer, contract, task order, or delivery order. The Basic, Medium, and High NIST SP 800-171 DoD Assessments are described in the NIST SP 800-171 DoD Assessment Methodology located at https://www.acq.osd.mil/asda/dpc/cp/cyber/safeguarding.html#nistSP800171"

3. **DFARS 252.204-7020 NIST SP 800-171 DoD Assessment Requirements**
   a. DFARS 252.204-7020(c): "The Contractor shall provide access to its facilities, systems, and personnel necessary for the Government to conduct a Medium or High NIST SP 800-171 DoD Assessment, as described in NIST SP 800-171 DoD Assessment Methodology at https://www.acq.osd.mil/asda/dpc/cp/cyber/safeguarding.html#nistSP800171, if necessary."

4. **DFARS 252.204-7021 Cybersecurity Maturity Model Certification Requirements**
   a. DFARS 252.204-7021(b): "The Contractor shall have a current (i.e. not older than 3 years) CMMC certificate at the CMMC level required by this contract and maintain the CMMC certificate at the required level for the duration of the contract." [This clause is what is currently going through the rulemaking process.]

Why

Question: Why was CMMC created?

There are several reasons why the DoD is establishing the CMMC program, but here are a few events that occurred, which have led the DoD to act:

- **July 22, 2004**
  - 'The 9/11 Commission Report' attributes the September 11 attacks to failure of federal agencies to share critical, unclassified information.

- **November 4, 2010**
  - President Barack Obama issues Executive Order 13556, establishing the CUI program.

- **October 21, 2016**
  - DFARS 252.204-7012 is published, establishing requirements for the Safeguarding of Covered Defense Information (CUI) and Cyber Incident Reporting.

- **March 26, 2019**
  - Hearing on the cybersecurity responsibilities of the defense industrial base, investigating the breach of CUI at a contractor for the Naval Undersea Warfare Center.

- **July 23, 2019**
  - Department of Defense Office of Inspector General published a report titled '*Audit of Protection of DoD Controlled Unclassified Information on Contractor-Owned Networks and Systems*'. It states, "DoD contractors *did not* consistently implement DoD-mandated system security controls for safeguarding Defense information."

- **February 22, 2022**
  - Department of Defense Office of Inspector General published a report titled '*Audit of the Protection of Military Research Information and Technologies Developed by Department of Defense Academic and Research Contractors*'. It states, "The 10 academic and research contractors we assessed *did not* consistently implement required cybersecurity controls to protect CUI stored on their networks from insider and external cyber threats."

- **September 7, 2022**
  - Defense News published an article titled '*Pentagon suspends F-35 deliveries over Chinese alloy in magnet*'. The Pentagon temporarily halted delivery of F-35 fighters following the discovery that the raw materials used for a magnet in the plane were produced in China.

- **October 5, 2022**
  - C4ISRNET published an article titled '*US says hackers attacked defense organization, stole sensitive info.*' Hackers infiltrated a defense industrial base organization, maintained "persistent, long-term" access to its network and absconded with sensitive data, U.S. government agencies said.

- **January 4, 2023**
  - CNN published an article titled '*CNN Exclusive: A single Iranian attack drone found to contain parts from more than a dozen US companies.*' Parts made by more than a dozen US and Western companies were found inside a single Iranian drone downed in Ukraine last fall, according to a Ukrainian intelligence assessment obtained exclusively by CNN.

How

Question: How can you prepare for CMMC?

Here are a few steps to get you started on your compliance journey:

1. Validate you have two things:
    a. The DFARS 252.204-7012 clause in your contractual agreement; and
    b. You are receiving CUI or generating CUI in the performance of a contract.

2. If both things are present, conduct a Basic self-assessment in accordance with DFARS 252.204-7019. You will need these two documents[3] to help with your self-assessment:
    a. NIST SP 800-171A / CMMC Level 2 Assessment Guide (The CMMC Level 2 Assessment Guide combines the discussion paragraphs from NIST SP 800-171 and the assessment objectives from NIST SP 800-171A).
    b. DoD Assessment Methodology v1.2.1

3. You will need to submit the following information into SPRS:
    a. System Security Plan
    b. CAGE Codes supported by this plan
    c. Brief description of the plan architecture
    d. Date of assessment
    e. Total score
    f. Date score of 110 will be achieved

4. Work towards remediating and closing out your POAM items.

---

[3] Refer to page 13 '*Tools*' for links to these documents.

The average time to achieve compliance is approximately 12-18 months. Most organizations do not have policies, procedures, compliant technologies and services, etc.

There is no such thing as a silver bullet, "one-size-fits-all", or "One-Stop Shop" solution to meet CMMC compliance. There are several administrative, technical, and physical control considerations that need to be made.

If you require professional assistance, you can identify consultants and others in the Cyber AB Marketplace to help you on your CMMC journey. As always, be sure to do your homework on any company you select to ensure both a good fit and avoid wasting precious time and resources.

Begin your journey TODAY!

Question: How can you get CMMC certified?

As of the writing of this publication, the DoD is still working on revisions to the final CMMC rule. If you've already invested the time and effort in becoming NIST SP 800-171 compliant, then the DoD's 'Joint Surveillance Voluntary Assessment', or JSVA, may be right for you. As stated in the name, these assessments are completely voluntary.

JSVA results are recorded as a DIBCAC High Assessment in the SPRS system. To be eligible for JSVA, you _must_ have at least one active DoD contract that includes the DFARS 252.204-7012 clause. Here's how it works:

- The contractor contracts a C3PAO and volunteers for JSVA.
- Your C3PAO will perform the NIST SP 800-171 portion of your assessment.
- The DIBCAC will perform the DFARS 252.204-7012 portion of your assessment, which consists of, but not limited to:
  - Verifying you have a medium-assurance certificate to report cyber incidents.
  - Verifying you are using a FedRAMP Moderate or equivalent cloud service provider and complies with paragraphs (c) through (g), assuming the cloud service provider is processing, storing, and/or transmitting CUI in performance of the contract.
  - Verifying you are flowing down the DFARS 252.204-7012 clause in accordance with paragraph (m) when subcontract performance involves covered defense information.
- If the contractor successfully passes their assessment, DIBCAC will enter the contractor's score in SPRS as a DIBCAC High Assessment.
- It is the DoD's intent that once CMMC rulemaking is completed, your DIBCAC High Assessment will convert to a CMMC certification and, at that time, your 3-year recertification clock would begin.

During an April 4th, 2023 webinar, Chief of Defense Industrial Base Cybersecurity Stacy Bostjanick stated, "Now I have to caveat this because it is our *intent*, if somebody throws a fit about this during rulemaking, which I don't know why anybody would, but our *intent* is if you go out and get a joint surveillance certification today, when the rule comes a thing and it's real, then your certification will be good for another three years after that, provided you've made those annual affirmations and those annual affirmations are made by somebody in the C-suite…"

If you have more questions about joint surveillance voluntary assessments, please reach out to a C3PAO on the Cyber AB Marketplace for more information.

Summary

CMMC is not a set of new controls. Rather, it is a third-party verification program of your existing requirements outlined in your DFARS 252.204-7012 contractual agreement.

I hope you have found this book informative and hopefully helped clarify some common misconceptions about the CMMC program.

CMMC ASSESSES _EXISTING_ REQUIREMENTS IN DFARS 7012

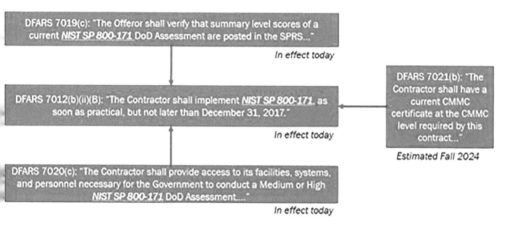

DFARS 7019(c): "The Offeror shall verify that summary level scores of a current _NIST SP 800-171_ DoD Assessment are posted in the SPRS..."

In effect today

DFARS 7021(b): "The Contractor shall have a current CMMC certificate at the CMMC level required by this contract..."

DFARS 7012(b)(ii)(B): "The Contractor shall implement _NIST SP 800-171_, as soon as practical, but not later than December 31, 2017."

In effect today

Estimated Fall 2024

DFARS 7020(c): "The Contractor shall provide access to its facilities, systems, and personnel necessary for the Government to conduct a Medium or High _NIST SP 800-171_ DoD Assessment...."

In effect today

About the Author

Fernando Machado is the Managing Principal and Chief Information Security Officer for Cybersec Investments, an Authorized CMMC 3rd Party Assessment Organization (C3PAO) and Service-Disabled Veteran-Owned Small Business (SDVOSB) located in Melbourne, Florida. Fernando is a Certified CMMC Assessor (CCA) and Certified CMMC Professional (CCP).

Fernando was an active member of early Cyber AB working groups and helped shape the CMMC training and certification programs, receiving recognition for his contributions with the President's Volunteer Service Award. He holds top cybersecurity industry certifications such as the Certified Information Systems Security Professional (CISSP), Certified Information Security Manager (CISM), Certified Information Systems Auditor (CISA), and more.

https://www.cybersecinvestments.com

Email: info@cybersecinvestments.com

Phone: (800) 960-8802

Printed in the USA
CPSIA information can be obtained
at www.ICGtesting.com
LVHW062131030424
776264LV00005B/38